RELIGIONS
of the Middle East

Gill Stacey

Academic Consultant:
William Ochsenwald
Professor of History, Virginia Polytechnic Institute
and State University

WORLD ALMANAC® LIBRARY

Please visit our website at: www.garethstevens.com
For a free color catalog describing World Almanac® Library's list of high-quality books and multimedia programs, call 1-800-848-2928 (USA) or 1-800-387-3178 (Canada). World Almanac® Library's Fax: (414) 332-3567.

Library of Congress Cataloging-in-Publication Data

Stacey, Gill
    Religions of the Middle East / Gill Stacey.
        p. cm. — (World Almanac Library of the Middle East)
    Includes bibliographical references and index.
    ISBN-10: 0-8368-7338-6 — ISBN-13: 978-0-8368-7338-2 (lib. bdg.)
    ISBN-10: 0-8368-7345-9 — ISBN-13: 978-0-8368-7345-0 (softcover)
    1. Middle East—Religion—Juvenile literature.   I. Title.   II. Series.
    BL1060.S73   2006
    200.956—dc22   2006014034

First published in 2007 by
World Almanac® Library
A Member of the WRC Media Family of Companies
330 West Olive Street, Suite 100
Milwaukee, WI 53212, USA

This edition © 2007 by World Almanac® Library.

Produced by Discovery Books
Editors: Geoff Barker, Amy Bauman, Paul Humphrey, and Gianna Quaglia
Series designer: Sabine Beaupré
Designer and page production: Ian Winton
Photo researcher: Rachel Tisdale
Maps and diagrams: Stefan Chabluk and Ian Winton
Academic Consultant: William Ochsenwald,
    Professor of History, Virginia Polytechnic Institute and
    State University
World Almanac® Library editorial direction: Mark J. Sachner
World Almanac® Library editor: Alan Wachtel
World Almanac® Library art direction: Tammy West
World Almanac® Library production: Jessica Morris

Photo credits: cover: Nabeel Turner/Stone/Getty Images; p. 5: AFP/Getty Images; p. 6: Karim Sahib/AFP/Getty Images; p. 13: Menahem Kahana/AFP/Getty Images; p. 15: Menahem Kahana/AFP/Getty Images; p. 17: David Silverman/Getty Images; p. 19: David Silverman/Getty Images; p. 21: David Silverman/Getty Images; p. 25: Norbert Schiller/Getty Images; p. 27: Joseph Barrak/AFP/Getty Images; p. 29: Muhannad Fala'ah/Getty Images; p. 31: Ghaith Abdul-Ahad/Getty Images; p. 34: Ahmad Al-Rubaye/AFP/Getty Images; p. 37: Gabriel Duval/AFP/Getty Images; p. 41: David Silverman/Getty Images.

Printed in the United States of America

1 2 3 4 5 6 7 8 9 10 09 08 07 06

CONTENTS

Cover: *An aerial view of the Great Mosque at Mecca, filled with pilgrims. All Muslims have a duty to visit Mecca at least once in their lifetime.*

The Middle East

The term *Middle East* has a long and complex history. It was originally used by the British in the nineteenth century to describe the area between the Near East (those lands gathered around the eastern end of the Mediterranean Sea) and Britain's empire in India. This area included Persia (later Iran), the **Mesopotamian provinces** of the **Ottoman Empire** (later Iraq), and the eastern half of Saudi Arabia. It was centered on the Persian Gulf.

The British had separate military commands for the Near East and the Middle East, but between the two world wars these commands were joined together. The new Middle East

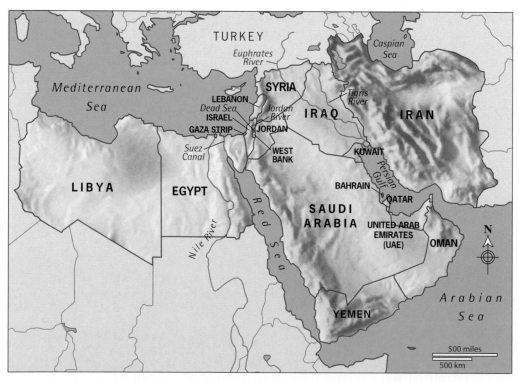

This map shows the fifteen countries of the Middle East that will be discussed in this book, as well as the West Bank and the Gaza Strip.

The late Pope John Paul II looks toward Jerusalem from Mount Nebo, Jordan, in 2000. Many sites in the Middle East are sacred to Christians, Jews, and Muslims alike.

Command included the old Near East Command, and stretched from Iran to Libya. After World War II, as the name *Middle East* became widely adopted, the term *Near East* fell out of use. By the end of the twentieth century, the term *Middle East* was in general use, both outside and inside the region itself. In this series, it is taken to include these fifteen countries: Libya and Egypt in north Africa; the Mediterranean coast countries of Israel, Lebanon, and Syria; Jordan, Iraq, and Iran; and the Arabian Peninsula countries of Bahrain, Kuwait, Saudi Arabia, United Arab Emirates, Oman, Yemen, and Qatar. It also includes the Arab Palestinian territories—the West Bank and Gaza Strip—which have had varying degrees of autonomy under Israeli occupation since 1967.

Why is this region important? Firstly, the Middle East has two-thirds of the fuel that keeps the rest of the world running—oil. Secondly, the Middle East was the original source of civilization.

The Middle East is also the birthplace of three great religions: Christianity, Judaism, and Islam. The Middle East includes Israel, the state of the Jewish people, and a significant proportion of the world's Muslims live in the region.

For these reasons, the affairs of the Middle East—its peoples and resources, religions and politics, revolutions and wars—are of vital interest to everyone on the planet.

CHAPTER 1

Birthplace of Three Major Religions

Three of the world's great **monotheistic** religions began in the Middle East: Judaism, Christianity, and Islam. This is not surprising, since the Middle East is often called the "cradle of civilization." For thousands of years, the Mediterranean Sea and the **Fertile Crescent** (the fertile cropland stretching in a crescent shape from the Nile Delta north along the Mediterranean coast

American tourists visit the famous ziggurat, a three-tiered monument dating from 2113 B.C., in the remains of the ancient city of Ur, the birthplace of Abraham. Ur is located in modern-day Iraq.

Zoroastrianism

The prophet Zoroaster was born in Persia (today's Iran) about 2,500 years ago. He became a priest in the polytheistic religion of the ancient Iranians and, through a series of visions, began to believe that there was only one God. The earliest **prophet** of any world religion, his teachings had a strong influence on the ideas developed later in Judaism, Christianity, and Islam. These included the ideas of a struggle between good and evil in the world, a final day of judgment, and the coming of a great leader or prophet to save the world.

Zoroastrianism was the official religion of the Persian empires until the arrival of Islam. Today, it has only a small number of followers, in Iran and other countries.

and east and southeast into the Tigris-Euphrates Valley) have encouraged people to settle, farm, and trade in this region. As settlements and trade grew, a people known as the Phoenicians developed the first known alphabet and some of the earliest towns and city states whose wealth was based on trade. These towns and trading networks allowed the development of larger and more powerful civilizations, including those of the Egyptians, Assyrians, Babylonians, and Persians, and later the Greeks and Romans. All these have left their imprint on the region, through their culture, languages, and religious beliefs.

The peoples of these ancient civilizations were **polytheistic**—that is, they worshipped many gods. With the development of writing, they began to record information about their religions, including creation stories and how stories of the gods related to one another and to humankind. It may be from this recording and listing of the gods and their different powers that the earliest concept of a more powerful god, possibly even a single god, began to develop. One of the first monotheistic religions to develop was Zoroastrianism. Although today it is one of the world's smallest religions, the beliefs and teachings of Zoroastrianism played a vital part in shaping the beliefs of Judaism, and, later, Christianity and Islam.

CHAPTER 2

Judaism

The Beginnings of Judaism
The roots of Judaism lie in the Middle Eastern region known as the Fertile Crescent (which today includes parts of Iraq, Syria, Jordan, Lebanon, and Israel, and the Palestinian territories). It began around four thousand years ago, the first of the major monotheistic religions to develop.

The ideas and beliefs at the core of Judaism developed gradually. There was no single founder, but Jews believe that two men played a very important part in shaping the early beliefs: Abraham and Moses.

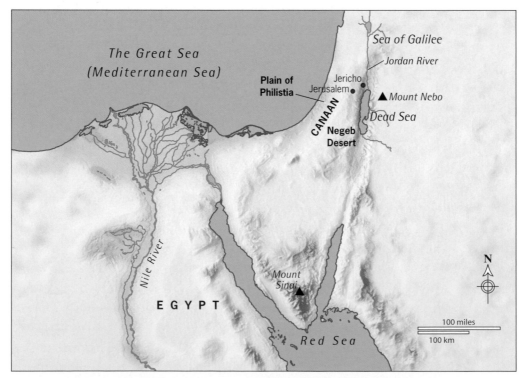

This map shows important places in the history of the Jews during the time of Moses.

8

Mount Nebo

Mount Nebo, in western Jordan, is a site of great religious significance to followers of Judaism, Christianity, and Islam, all of whom revere Moses as a prophet. They believe that Moses climbed Mount Nebo to see the land of Canaan before he died. Jewish and Christian traditions say that Moses was buried on the mountain; Muslims believe that his body was carried across the Jordan River for burial.

Early Prophets: Abraham and Moses

According to the Jewish holy books, Abraham and his family lived in the city of Ur (in modern-day Iraq), where the people worshipped many gods. Abraham became convinced this was wrong and that there was only one God. Jewish teaching suggests that, probably around 2000 B.C., God told Abraham to travel to a land called Canaan (roughly where Israel is today). Here, Jews believe, God promised Abraham that he would be the father of a great nation and that this land would belong to his descendants forever. This, they believe, was the beginning of the **covenant**, the special relationship that Jews believe they have with God.

The Jewish holy books also tell how famine forced Abraham's descendants to leave Canaan and seek refuge in Egypt, where they became known as the Israelites. In the thirteenth century B.C., after suffering cruel enslavement by the ancient Egyptians, the Israelites began the Exodus, their long journey back to Canaan. Jews believe that God chose Moses to lead his people back to the Promised Land. For nearly forty years, the Israelites lived as nomads in the desert. During this time, Moses spent forty days and nights on Mount Sinai (located on the Sinai Peninsula in northeastern Egypt), where the Jewish holy books say God revealed more of the covenant to him: he would take special care of the Jews as long as they obeyed his laws, the most important of which are the Ten Commandments.

It was under Moses' successor, Joshua, that the Israelites finally reached Canaan. Many years of war with the peoples already living there followed before the Israelites were able to take back the land.

Leaving the Promised Land

The land of the Israelites was invaded by successive, powerful empires, including the Babylonians in 586 B.C. and the Romans in 63 B.C. From the time of the Babylonians, large numbers of Jews left their land, as a result of being forced or to escape enemy rule. In A.D. 70, the Romans expelled all Jews from Judaea, as the Roman province in Palestine was called, and Jewish communities fled to other lands of the Roman Empire and beyond. This dispersal became known as the **Diaspora**. Few Jews were to return to the lands of their ancestors until the twentieth century.

Persecution in Europe

In the centuries that followed, the Jews had to fight to hold onto their identity. They were frequently persecuted and often forced to live in **ghettos**, particularly in Christian European countries. This persecution culminated in the Nazi **Holocaust** of World War II (1939–1945), when six million Jews were killed. After the war, the **Zionist** movement, which had begun in the late nineteenth century, intensified its campaign for a Jewish state in the Jews' ancient homeland in the region of Palestine, where they could live and worship without fear of persecution. In 1948, the state of Israel was declared, and many thousands of Jews of the Diaspora emigrated to Israel. Today, Israel's population of more than six million is 80 percent Jewish.

Judaism in the Middle East

While some Jewish communities have been present in the Middle East since before the birth of Jesus Christ, other communities were founded later by Jews of the Diaspora, and still others developed as refugees fled persecution in Europe in the twentieth century. In general, Jews found more tolerance in these largely Muslim lands than in Europe. However, their position could be **precarious**. Under intolerant rulers or during times of political instability, Middle Eastern Jews often suffered serious discrimination. Under more stable conditions, they were often able to attain important positions in the wider society.

The Jews—and people of other minority communities, such as the Christians—were often given the status of *dhimmis*. Under Muslim law, dhimmis had limited rights, including the right to follow their own religious practices and laws, provided they recognized Muslim authority and paid special taxes. Most spoke Arabic and differed little in appearance from their Arab neighbors. They were often successful traders, businesspeople, or craftspeople. However, they took care to be discreet about their religious practices or any wealth they accumulated to avoid conflict with Muslims.

Tiny Communities

It is estimated that, until 1948 and the establishment of the state of Israel, about one million Jews lived throughout the Middle Eastern Muslim countries. Today, many of these Jewish communities are so tiny that they are expected to die out in the near future. In Egypt, for example, a Jewish community that dates back over three thousand years is now estimated at fewer than two hundred people. Most of the members of these groups left either because they were actively encouraged by Jewish organizations to settle in Israel or because they feared persecution with the rise of anti-Jewish feeling among Muslims.

Yemeni Jews

There have been Jewish settlements in Yemen for at least two thousand years. At different times under Muslim rule, Yemeni Jews suffered discrimination and sometimes enforced exile. Over the centuries, however, they have continued to play a vital part in the country's economy. Isolated from other Jewish communities in other Middle Eastern countries, they developed a distinctive Yemeni Jewish culture, absorbing influences from the Yemeni Arabs.

After the establishment of Israel in 1948, the Israeli authorities actively encouraged Jews to settle in the new homeland. About fifty thousand Yemeni Jews were airlifted to Israel, leaving behind tiny remnants of their original communities.

Core Beliefs and Teachings

According to Jewish belief, there is only one God, and he is eternal. He created everything and is everywhere. The Jewish concept of a single, all-powerful God played an important part in shaping the core beliefs of Christianity and Islam. Jews believe that they are God's "chosen people" and that they have a covenant with God. Central to this covenant are the Ten Commandments, which they believe God gave to Moses and which are the basis of Judaism.

Some Jews believe that, one day, a **Messiah** (the "anointed one") will finally deliver them from their enemies and establish God's kingdom of love and peace on Earth. But not all Jews adhere to this belief. Others believe that it is up to humankind to unite to establish this Earthly kingdom.

The Jewish Holy Books

The Jewish scriptures, known as the Tanakh, are a collection of books divided into three sections: the Torah (the teachings), the Nevi'im (the prophets), and the Ketuvim (the writings). These books were written in Hebrew over many centuries by different authors.

The main teachings of Judaism are contained in the Torah. This includes the five books of Moses—Genesis, Exodus, Leviticus, Numbers, and Deuteronomy—and it tells the story of the Jewish people from the time of Abraham to the death of Moses. Jews believe that the Torah contains instructions from God as to how they should live, including his requirement that they follow the Ten Commandments.

The Nevi'im includes the books believed to have been

Being Jewish

According to Jewish tradition, anyone who has a Jewish mother is a Jew. There are also people who have chosen to convert to Judaism, but, unlike Christianity and Islam, Judaism does not actively seek converts. Not all Jews observe the practices of Judaism, and those who do may follow the religion in different ways. Most Jews, however, have a strong sense of their identity, of being part of the wider Jewish community, and of a shared religious and cultural heritage.

Ultra-Orthodox Jews in Netanya, Israel, celebrate the festival of Purim in their local synagogue.

written by God's prophets, who explained the meaning of events in Jewish history and warned about the dangers of disobeying God. The Ketuvim includes the Book of Psalms, said to have been written by King David, who was regarded by many Jews as their greatest king.

In addition, Jews also study the Talmud, a collection of detailed teachings that give guidance on a wide variety of topics, including law, religious practices, and everyday life.

Worship

Jews can worship at home or in a **synagogue**. There are synagogue services every day, although many observant Jews attend most frequently on the morning of the Sabbath (*Shabbat* in Hebrew). The Sabbath celebrates the seventh day, during which God rested after creating the world. It begins at sunset on Friday and continues until the stars appear on Saturday. Strict Jews will do no work on the Sabbath, including cooking and driving.

During a synagogue service, psalms are recited or sung, and members of the congregation are chosen to give readings from the Torah. The congregation recites the Shema, the most important Jewish prayer.

Prayers in the synagogue are often led by the rabbi, the spiritual leader for the Jewish community. Rabbis also teach the community, especially the children, about Judaism. They also advise on Jewish law. Most rabbis are men, although in the Reform movement women can also become rabbis.

Jewish Festivals

The Jewish year includes many festivals. Some of these celebrations recall important events in Jewish history; others are linked to the seasons. They usually include special services at the synagogue, as well as family ceremonies and meals.

The festival of Rosh Hashanah marks the Jewish New Year and is celebrated in late September or early October. It also marks the beginning of the most solemn period of the Jewish year—the days of repentance. During these ten days, Jews reflect on the past year and seek to put their lives in order. This period ends with Yom Kippur, the Day of Atonement, the most solemn day of the Jewish year, which is spent in fasting and prayer.

This is followed by the festival of Sukkot, when Jews remember the time spent in the wilderness during the Exodus. Many families collect branches and leaves to make special tents, called sukkot. The word *sukkot* (or *sukkah* in singular) means "booths" in Hebrew and reminds the Jews of the temporary shelters they used when they had no settled homes. In Jerusalem, processions of worshippers carry bundles of palm, myrtle, and willow, as directed by the Torah, together with the scrolls of the Torah to the Wailing Wall, while singing in Hebrew.

In December, Hanukkah is celebrated with lights and rejoicing. It reminds Jews of when their ancestors recaptured the Holy

THE JEWISH CALENDAR

September/October	Rosh Hashanah	Jewish New Year
October	Yom Kippur	Day of Atonement
October	Sukkot	Feast of Tabernacles
December	Hanukkah	Festival of Light
March	Purim	Deliverance in Persia
March/April	Passover (Pesach)	Exodus from Egypt

Jewish festivals, like the Christian festival of Easter and like Muslim holidays, are moveable. They do not occur on the same day every year because they follow a lunar calendar.

Survivors

"We are an ancient people, twice as old as Christianity, three times as old as Islam. And if history teaches us anything, it is this, that Judaism survives not by numbers but by the quality and strength of Jewish faith. We always were an obstinate people, too obstinate to let go of God, too obstinate to be defeated by history."

Jonathan Sacks, Chief Rabbi of the United Hebrew Congregations of the British Commonwealth, 2001.

Temple in Jerusalem over two thousand years ago. At that time, according to the story, the Jews could find only enough oil to burn the holy temple light for one day. The light is believed to have continued burning—miraculously—for eight days.

Passover, or Pesach, is celebrated in March or April. At this time, Jews remember the beginning of the Exodus from Egypt, when Moses led them to freedom. Special foods, which have symbolic meanings, are eaten at this time. One of the most important of these is **matzo**, which reminds Jews that they had to flee Egypt in haste without enough time for the dough to rise for the next day's bread.

Ethiopian Jews hold a traditional colorful umbrella during the Jewish holiday of Sukkot while celebrating at the Western Wall, in Jerusalem. Many Ethiopian Jews emigrated to Israel in the late 1980s.

Orthodox and Non-Orthodox Jews

Within Judaism there are different movements. These can broadly be divided into two main groups: Orthodox and non-Orthodox.

At the heart of Orthodox Judaism is the belief that the Torah is the word of God and cannot be changed in any way. Orthodox Jews are strict about following traditional Jewish laws. Men and women have different roles. Men play a more important part in the wider world, especially in the synagogue. Women sit apart from the men, do not take part in the service, and are not allowed to become rabbis. However, women are in charge of the family home, an important institution in Judaism.

There are different subgroups within Orthodox Judaism— and these are represented in different ways in Israel. The ultra-Orthodox (or *haredi*) reject the modern world and live separately within their own communities. They live a very strict life according to the word of the Talmud, the Jewish books of civil and religious tradition. In many ways, they are outside the state. For example, they are not drafted into the army as all other Israeli Jews are, and some extreme groups of haredi even

Secular Versus Orthodox

After Israel was founded in 1948, Orthodox religious laws were built into the state system. Civil marriages were prohibited, and the Sabbath and *kashruth* (special dietary laws) had to be observed. Orthodox Jews were given special privileges, including separate education (often in religious schools, known as *yeshivot*) with state funding. More recently, small Orthodox political parties have also wielded considerable power in Israel's system of coalition government.

As the population of Israel has grown and changed, the disproportionate influence of the Orthodox minority has caused considerable resentment among the non-Orthodox and secular majority. In recent years, Israel's courts have introduced reforms to reduce Orthodox privileges. In 2005, Israel's Supreme Court ended the Orthodox monopoly on **conversions** to Judaism in Israel. In response, Orthodox rabbis have angrily accused the courts of trying to destroy Judaism and their way of life.

Ultra-Orthodox Jews go shopping in Jerusalem for myrtle leaves, which are used in the festival of Sukkot.

reject the state of Israel, which they regard as **heretical**. An estimated 135,000 haredi Jews live in the city of Jerusalem today. In contrast, modern Orthodox, or neo-Orthodox, Jews are committed to the state of Israel and take part in all aspects of Israeli life.

Hasidic Jews make up an important group within the Orthodox movement. This group began in eighteenth-century Poland, and most of its members still wear traditional dress from that time. The Hasidic Jews were almost wiped out during the Holocaust, and many of the group's survivors emigrated to Israel.

Non-Orthodox Jews include several groups. The largest of these groups is probably the Reform Jews, who have adapted their religious practices to modern life and who reject the more rigid traditions of the Orthodox movements. They believe that the Torah is inspired by God, rather than the actual words of God. There are also Conservative Jews, who follow traditional religious practices but are closer to Reform Jews in their beliefs and attitudes to modern society. In Israel, these newer movements have attracted fewer followers than in the United States and Europe.

In addition, there are **secular** Jews, who do not follow the religious laws of Judaism. For secular Jews, what is important about being Jewish are Jewish values and culture. Many Jews are also secular Zionists, stressing the importance of the Jewish nation state in contrast to Orthodox Zionists, who believe in the return to the land that God promised to Abraham. Approximately 70 percent of Israeli Jews are secular Jews.

CHAPTER 3

Christianity

The Beginnings of Christianity

Christianity began about two thousand years ago in Palestine, which was then part of the Roman Empire. The founders were the first followers of Jesus Christ, who they believed was the Messiah predicted in the Jewish **scriptures**.

Jesus was born into a Jewish family that was living in Palestine about 6 B.C. Little is known of Jesus' childhood, but we do know that he was brought up and educated according to Jewish laws and customs. About the time he turned thirty, Jesus was **baptized** by a wandering preacher known as John the Baptist, who believed that Jesus was the long-awaited Messiah.

The Baptism Site

In the 1990s, archaeologists began excavating a long-lost settlement known as Bethany-beyond-the-Jordan, near Jordan's western border with Israel. What the scientists found here, supported by evidence in the Bible and other written sources, convinced them that this was probably the most important religious and archaeological discovery of modern times: the place where John the Baptist had lived and preached nearly two thousand years ago, and where he had baptized Jesus.

Along the banks of the Jordan River, archaeologists discovered a series of baptism pools. Their finds also revealed that, for possibly hundreds of years, Bethany was a major religious site for Christian **pilgrims**. These finds included the remains of several Byzantine churches, **hermits**' caves, and lodgings for pilgrims, as well as written records of those who stayed there.

Russian-Orthodox Christian pilgrims baptize themselves during Epiphany celebrations in the murky waters of the Jordan River near Jericho, in the West Bank. Every year thousands of pilgrims gather at the site where Eastern churches believe Jesus was baptized by John the Baptist.

After his baptism, Jesus spent the rest of his short life teaching and spreading the word of God. He gathered twelve devoted **disciples** around him—ordinary men who gave up their everyday lives to follow him. Thousands came to hear his message. The Christian holy books report that he performed many miracles—healing the sick, calming raging storms, and turning water into wine—that showed his special powers and confirmed to followers that he was the Messiah.

However, what Jesus said and did brought him into conflict with Jewish religious leaders. They did not believe he was the Messiah and accused him of claiming to be a king. The Roman authorities were also worried by Jesus' growing popularity. Although there was no evidence against him, Jesus was brought to trial before the Roman governor, Pontius Pilate, and sentenced to death by **crucifixion**.

After Jesus' death, his body was sealed up in a tomb made of rock. His disciples were heartbroken; this was the end of everything they had waited for and believed in. Then, in the weeks that followed, the Christian holy books claim that the disciples saw and spoke to Jesus on several occasions. They believed that he had risen from the dead—the **Resurrection**. They also believed that, forty days after his death, they saw Jesus ascend to Heaven to be reunited with God.

The Spread of Christianity

After Jesus died, his followers began to travel widely, preaching the Christian message. In these early years, they were a small **sect**, an offshoot of Judaism. They suffered great persecution, particularly by the Roman authorities. But the strong beliefs of Jesus' followers endured. Just over three hundred years after his death, the Roman Emperor Constantine converted to Christianity, and this religion became the accepted faith throughout the empire. Until the arrival of Islam in the seventh century, it was the most important religion in the lands near Jesus' birthplace—lands that today make up Syria, Jordan, Israel, the West Bank, the Gaza Strip, and Egypt. Many of the Christians in the Middle East today are descendants of those early converts.

A Middle Eastern Religion

"I keep reminding people that Christianity started in Palestine. It's a Middle Eastern religion, and we are extensions of the earliest community in Palestine. We have been there for centuries. . . . We are Palestinians, and we happened to be Christians, and this is part of our heritage and our authenticity."

Dr. Hanan Ashrawi, an Anglican Christian and spokesperson for the Palestinian delegation to the Israel/Palestinian peace talks (Commonweal, October 8, 1993).

Divisions within Christianity

Over the centuries, as Christianity grew and spread, it broke up into a number of different **denominations**, or churches. Broadly, these fall into three groups: Orthodox, Protestant, and Roman Catholic. There are also many subdivisions of these groups, many of which are represented in Middle Eastern countries today.

The first main division within Christianity came about in the fifth century, when people began to disagree about the nature of Jesus. Some Christians believed that Jesus was both human and divine, while others believed that he was solely divine. In the eleventh century, there was serious disagreement between the pope, who led the western church from Rome, and the **patriarch** of Constantinople, who led the eastern church. These two leaders accused each other of false beliefs and disagreed over who had the greater authority. This led to a split known as the Great Schism, which was to have a lasting effect upon Christianity in the Middle East. The eastern part of the Christian church became known as the Orthodox Church; the western part became the Roman Catholic Church. In the sixteenth century, a movement known as the **Reformation** divided the western church into Roman Catholic and Protestant denominations.

Christianity in the Middle East Today

The majority of Christians in the Middle East live in countries where, in terms of their religion, they are a minority. Most are Arabs; they have a strong sense of Arab identity, and speak Arabic as their first language. They have lived alongside their Muslim neighbors for hundreds of years.

In most Middle Eastern countries, Islam is the official religion. Nevertheless, Christians are generally recognized by national governments as official religious minorities. They are subject to the civil laws of the country but may follow their own religious laws with regard to marriage, divorce, and inheritance.

A Palestinian Christian woman and her daughters use Arabic-language prayer books as they pray in St. Catherine's Church in the West Bank town of Bethlehem.

In strict Islamic societies such as Iran, Christians have been expected to observe certain Islamic laws, such as wearing modest dress, avoiding alcohol, and maintaining the separation of the sexes in public. Such expectations have often caused resentment, particularly when they prevent Christians from following their traditional religious practices, such as sharing bread and wine during Holy Communion.

Most Middle Eastern Christians are urban dwellers. Many are well educated and successful. Children in Christian families in the Middle East are more likely to attend private faith-based schools than those from Muslim families.

Core Beliefs and Teachings

All Christians, whatever their denomination, share the same core beliefs. Christians believe in one all-powerful and all-seeing God. They believe God exists in three forms: God the Father, God the Son, and God the Holy Spirit. God the Father created the heavens, Earth, and everything that lives. Christians also believe that Jesus is the Son of God, who was sent to Earth to save humankind. The Holy Spirit is seen as the spirit of God, who continues God's work on Earth.

The life and teachings of Jesus are at the heart of Christian belief. Christians believe that the sacrifice God made in giving up his son to death on the cross shows how much God loves all people. Christians take comfort from Jesus' resurrection and **ascension**, believing that death is not the end but an entry into a new life. Christianity says that those who believe in Jesus and his power to forgive their sins will ascend to heaven.

The Christian Holy Book: The Bible

The Christian Bible is in fact a collection of books written by different authors. The largest part of this collection is the Old Testament, which contains writings from the Jewish holy books, the Torah, the Nevi'im, and the Ketuvim. Most of the New Testament books were written in the first century A.D. by Christians who were the early followers of Jesus. The most-loved books of the New Testament are the four Gospels, which tell of Jesus' life and teachings. The later books of the New Testament were written by early church leaders, giving

Bethlehem

For centuries, the town of Bethlehem has been revered by Christians as the birthplace of Jesus, and pilgrims have flocked there at Christmas. For centuries, it has also been fought over by Jews, Christians, and Muslims. Today, Bethlehem is part of the Palestinian territories, with a population of around thirty thousand people. Although Christians originally dominated there, their numbers have dwindled, particularly over the last decade. Several sources report that Muslims now make up the majority. Recent conflicts between the Palestinians and the Israelis have put Bethlehem under occupation and curfew. Fewer pilgrims now visit, and many Christians see little future there.

guidance and comfort to the small, persecuted Christian community. They include the letters from St. Paul.

Worship

Christians meet to worship in a church. Services are often held in church during the week, but the main day for worship is Sunday. Sunday is special for Christians because they believe that this is the day when Jesus rose from the dead.

Church services are led by a priest, the spiritual leader for the local Christian community. Priests are guided by more senior figures, known as bishops. At the head of the church, different denominations look to different leaders. For example, Roman Catholics have one leader, the pope; the Orthodox Churches each have a leader called a patriarch.

During a Christian service, the worshippers say prayers and sing hymns in praise of God. Both the priest and other worshippers read from the Bible, and the priest gives a sermon, or talk, about the meaning of Jesus' teachings. The service may also include a special act of worship, the **Eucharist,** or Holy Communion, during which Christians remember and honor the Last Supper that Jesus shared with his disciples before his death. Roman Catholics call this celebration Mass; in Orthodox Churches, it is known as the Holy Liturgy.

Christian Festivals

Most Christian festivals celebrate events in the life of Jesus Christ. The most important are Christmas and Easter.

Christmas honors the birth of Jesus and is a time of special joy for Christians. Christmas is celebrated on December 25 in Roman Catholic and Protestant Churches and on January 7 in Orthodox Churches. At midnight on Christmas Eve, many Christians attend special church services. The festival is also a time for sharing with family and friends, feasting, and exchanging presents.

Easter is probably the most important festival for Christians in the Middle East, especially those who belong to Orthodox churches. Before Easter, many people fast during the period known as Lent. Lent, which runs for forty weekdays before Easter, is meant to remind Christians how Jesus suffered alone in the desert for forty days before he began his teaching. Good Friday, which is the last Friday in Lent, is a day of mourning and prayer, recalling Jesus' crucifixion. Families attend church for Easter Mass at midnight on Saturday or on Sunday morning, in preparation for Easter Sunday, when they believe Jesus rose from the dead. On this day, people prepare special foods and visit as many friends and family as they can.

Christians in Israel celebrate Christmas and Easter by making pilgrimages to the holy sites. They are joined by Christian pilgrims from around the world. In Lebanon, villages that have large majority Christian populations have their own patron saints and celebrate saints' days at different times throughout the year. Villagers may decorate their local church and hold processions carrying an effigy of their local patron saint.

The Orthodox Church

The majority of Middle Eastern Christians belong to subdivisions of the eastern Orthodox Church. These include the Coptic, Syrian, and Armenian Orthodox Churches, whose followers believe that Jesus Christ had a single, divine nature, and the Greek and Assyrian Orthodox Churches, whose followers believe he was both human *and* divine.

The Coptic Church is the largest Christian church in the Middle East. The majority of Copts live in Egypt, where they

An Egyptian priest administers Holy Communion during a Palm Sunday service at the Coptic Orthodox Church of Saint Samaan in Cairo, Egypt.

make up an estimated 10 percent of the population. Copts claim descent from the ancient Egyptians; they are ethnically the same as other Egyptians but culturally distinct. Their church is one of the oldest in the Christian world. Copts themselves believe their church began with Mark, one of Jesus' disciples. The head of the Coptic Church is the patriarch of Alexandria, who is based in Cairo. The Copts hold their services in Arabic and in Coptic. The Coptic language is a form of the ancient Egyptian language and was spoken during early Christian times.

Followers of the Syrian Orthodox Church (also known as Jacobites) are found mostly in Lebanon and Syria. They worship in Syriac, a dialect of ancient Aramaic, the main language of the Middle East before Arabic, and the language spoken by Jesus. In worship, they make the sign of the cross with one finger, signifying their belief in Jesus' single, divine nature. Their spiritual leader is the patriarch of Antioch, who is located in Damascus, Syria.

The Armenians make up one of the few Middle Eastern Christian groups that are not Arabs. Christian Armenian communities have existed in the Middle East for centuries, but most arrived in the region in the first half of the twentieth century, fleeing persecution by the Turks. Both Armenian Orthodox and Armenian Catholic Churches hold their services in classical Armenian and strongly guard their national traditions and identity. They live mainly in Iran, Syria, Lebanon, and Jordan.

Followers of the Greek Orthodox Church can be found throughout much of the Middle East, including Egypt, Israel, the Palestinian territories, Lebanon, Syria, and Jordan. Most of these Christians are Arabs, although in Egypt the majority of them are of Greek origin. Either Greek or Arabic may be used in worship, and leaders are patriarchs based in Alexandria in Egypt, Damascus, and Jerusalem.

Members of the Assyrian Orthodox Church (sometimes called Nestorians) worship in the Syriac language, in simple churches with little decoration. This church's members live mainly in Lebanon, Syria, Iran, and Iraq.

The Uniate Churches

The Uniates have their origins in the eastern Orthodox Church but reestablished their link with the Roman Catholic Church in the twelfth century or later by accepting the pope in Rome as their supreme spiritual leader. This group of churches is found mostly in Lebanon and Syria, and includes the Maronites and the Greek and Syrian Catholics. Uniates continue to use traditional or local languages in their services, such as Arabic or Syriac, and their priests are allowed to marry (in contrast with Roman Catholic priests, who cannot).

Other Christian Denominations

The Middle East is also home to Christians belonging to Western churches such as the Roman Catholic, Protestant, and Anglican Churches, but these groups have smaller numbers. Protestant denominations in the Middle East include Presbyterians and Episcopalians. These Christians are found in Syria, Lebanon, Egypt, Iran, Jordan, Israel, and the Palestinian territories. Almost all of these people are relatively recent converts through the work of American and European **missionaries** in the nineteenth and twentieth centuries. Most of these converts have come from other Christian churches; very few have a Muslim background.

Members of Western denominations are more likely to suffer discrimination in Muslim countries than those in the more established Eastern churches. In the Islamic Republic of Iran, for example, minority religions are recognized by the

The Maronites

The Maronite Church traces its origins back to a fourth-century monk, St. Maron, who lived in Syria. Persecuted for their beliefs, the Maronites later sought refuge in the rough terrain of the mountains of Syria and Lebanon. For several hundred years, these mountains became their power base, where they developed as isolated, fiercely independent communities.

In the twentieth century, the Maronites became very powerful in Lebanon. The political system established in the 1930s placed them in a dominant position, which later brought them into conflict with Lebanese Muslims, in particular the Druze, during the Lebanese Civil War (1975–1991).

The Maronites still play an important role in the economy and politics of Lebanon. However, the group's power and influence have diminished, and significant numbers of its members have emigrated in search of a more secure life in the West.

constitution, and Christians hold a small number of reserved seats in parliament. Yet, under Iranian law, conversion from Islam to any other faith is a crime, and well-documented reports describe the ill-treatment of some Christians, especially those belonging to **evangelical** churches.

A Lebanese woman prays at the Maronite church of Saint Sharbel in the mountain village of Ennaya, located northeast of Beirut, Lebanon. The portrait behind her is of Saint Maron.

CHAPTER 4

Islam

The Beginnings of Islam

Islam began in Arabia (in modern-day Saudi Arabia) in the seventh century A.D. Followers of Islam, however, believe that their religion was created by God, whom they call Allah, at the very beginning of time, and that the word of Allah was revealed to the world through a series of messengers, including Adam ("the first Muslim"), Abraham, Moses, and Jesus. These messengers, or prophets, are also found in the Jewish Torah and the Christian Bible. However, for Muslims, the most important messenger was the one they believe to be the final one, Muhammad.

Muhammad was born in the Arabian city of Mecca in A.D. 570. From a poor background and orphaned when he was young, Muhammad became a successful trader with a reputation for hard work and honesty. A deeply spiritual man, Muslims believe he began to receive **revelations** from Allah through the

Mecca and Medina

Today, the cities (in modern-day Saudi Arabia) where Islam began are two of the three holiest cities of Islam (the other being Jerusalem). Mecca, in particular, is sacred because it was here, Muslims believe, that Muhammad had his first revelations. Every year, during the twelfth month of the Islamic calendar, pilgrims from all over the Islamic world flock to Mecca. For these Muslim pilgrims the *hajj* to Mecca is a deeply spiritual experience that they believe brings them closer to Allah. All pilgrims dress and live very simply and devoutly during this time, showing that all Muslims are equal before Allah.

angel Gabriel. These revelations were written down after Muhammad's death and form the Muslim holy book, the Koran.

In 613, Muhammad began to preach Allah's message to the people of Mecca, condemning their worship of **pagan** gods. Rejection and ill-treatment forced Muhammad, along with a small group of loyal followers, to flee to the city of Medina in 622. This flight became known as the *hijrah* and marks the beginning of the Islamic era. Medina was to become the first Muslim city, with Muhammad as its ruler. In 630, he returned to Mecca with many thousands of followers and threw the pagan **idols** out of the Ka'ba, the sacred house said to have been built by Abraham. Muhammad died in 632, leaving no clear successor. The survival of the fledgling faith was uncertain and its future direction unclear.

Thousands of Muslim pilgrims circle around the holy Ka'ba, located in the Grand Mosque, during the hajj in the holy city of Mecca, Saudi Arabia.

The Spread of Islam

After Muhammad's death, his trusted follower Abu Bakr was chosen as Caliph (deputy or successor), and under his leadership, Islam spread through the whole of Arabia. In less than one hundred years, often through conquest, it became the dominant religion in the Middle East and North Africa.

Abu Bakr was succeeded in turn by Umar, Uthman, and Ali, all companions of Muhammad and known collectively as the four Caliphs. In 661, not long after the death of Ali—Muhammad's cousin and son-in-law—the Muslim community split into two groups. The two new groups, called the Sunnis and the Shi'as, disagreed over who should rightfully lead the Muslim community.

Core Beliefs and Teachings

Muslims believe that Allah is the one and only God, and that he created everything. They also believe that Muhammad was the final and most important of many messengers sent to reveal the word of Allah to humankind.

Muslims are taught to submit completely to the will of Allah and to follow the Five Pillars of Islam. These five duties govern every aspect of Muslim life and unite all Muslims, no matter where they live in the world, into a single community, known as *ummah*. The Five Pillars are *shahada* (creed), *salat* (prayer), *zakat* (almsgiving), *saum* (fasting), and hajj (pilgrimage). The most important of these is shahada, the declaration of faith, and Muslims say it thousands of times during their lives: "There is no God but Allah, and Muhammad is his messenger." According to Islamic practice, all Muslims should say this prayer, in Arabic, five times a day facing toward Mecca.

Zakat, or giving to the poor, is regarded as a spiritual act. Every Muslim is expected to give at least 2.5 percent of the money he or she accumulates over a year. Muslims believe that saum, or fasting, helps them develop self-control, religious understanding, and compassion. During the holy month of Ramadan, for example, Muslims try to lead pure lives, helping one another, as well as submitting to the discipline of fasting. Every healthy Muslim is expected to fast at this time and must not eat or drink between dawn and sunset. The hajj is the pilgrimage to Mecca—a trip that all Muslims hope to make at least once in their lifetimes.

Islamic Religious Schools

In most Middle Eastern countries, Islamic religious schools, called *madrasas*, exist alongside the largely secular state education system. Often attached to mosques, the schools lead their students in the study of Islamic texts, above all the Koran and the Hadith. Educational methods are rote, involving memorization of verses from the Koran. The schools are attended mostly by boys, although a few madrasas are designed specifically for girls.

Attending a madrasa is free, because they are funded by donations from the Muslim community. In recent years, a shortage of good state schools has encouraged more parents, especially those in poorer communities, to send their children to madrasas. Some madrasas have been accused of encouraging a militant, anti-Western form of Islam, particularly in Yemen and in Saudi Arabia.

A teacher instructs female students at a madrasa, an Islamic school, in Baghdad.

Sharia

The foundations of sharia, the Islamic system of law, were developed in the eighth century by Muslim scholars. Sharia is regarded as sacred and is based on the teachings of Muhammad. Sharia law provides a code for all aspects of a Muslim's life, including marriage, divorce, prayers, dress, and dietary restrictions, as well as rules against criminal acts such as theft or murder.

Sharia is an important legal influence throughout the Islamic world, but the ways in which it is applied vary greatly. In most Middle Eastern countries, sharia is applied selectively. For example, the criminal justice systems of countries such as Jordan, Egypt, Lebanon, and Syria do not include *hudud* laws, which specify severe penalties for particular crimes. These penalties include beatings with a lash for drinking alcohol, the amputation of limbs for theft, and the stoning of adulterers.

In those countries governed by strict Islamic regimes, such as Saudi Arabia and Iran, a more rigid interpretation of sharia is the supreme law of the land. Saudi Arabia has long handed out harsh penalties, or hudud, including public executions and lashings. More recently, in some Middle Eastern countries with largely secular governments, Islamic leaders have begun to advocate a return to a more "pure" sharia.

Sharia is often seen as discriminating against women. For example, in some applications of sharia, a woman's testimony in court is worth half that of a man's. But some Muslim scholars argue that Islam places great emphasis on justice and equality, and that discrimination stems from incorrect interpretation of the law, usually by men. In Iran, Shirin Ebadi, a lawyer who became the country's first female judge in the 1970s, has used

Women Fighting for Justice

"The head of the court told me I could not work as a judge because I am a woman. He said it was forbidden by sharia law. . . . We have been fed so many things in the name of Islam and sharia law."

Shirin Ebadi, Iran, winner of the Nobel Peace Prize, 2003.

sharia law to fight for the rights of women and children, particularly with regard to divorce and inheritance laws.

The Koran and the Hadith

Muslims believe that all the important teachings of Islam are contained in the Koran, the words of which are believed to be the actual words of Allah. The Koran is divided into 114 *suras*, or chapters, which give guidance on all aspects of religion and everyday life. These suras show Muslims how to live in total submission to Allah and prepare for the coming Day of Judgment. The words of the Koran cannot be changed or interpreted, so all Muslims prefer to read and recite the Koran in the original Arabic.

The *hadith* are a collection of stories and sayings from the life and teachings of Muhammad. The hadith are open to discussion in a way that the Koran is not. They are often consulted to clarify areas that the Koran does not make clear. For example, hadith are consulted in legal decisions.

Worship

Muslims can pray to Allah anywhere, but often they will go to a mosque to do so. A mosque is a center of Islamic learning as well as prayer and is the heart of a Muslim community. Many Muslims try to attend mosque every day, but they make a special effort to go for Friday prayers, when the imam, or prayer leader, gives a sermon. In Islam, men and women pray separately. Before praying, worshippers must wash their face, arms, head, and feet. Then they must follow a precise order of movements including standing, bowing, kneeling, and placing their foreheads on the ground.

There are no ordained priests in Islam (in contrast with Christianity). Muslims believe that all guidance comes from Allah and can be found in the teachings of the Koran and the hadith. The imam who leads prayers is usually very learned in the teachings of the Koran. He may be called upon to advise members of the Muslim community if they have questions or problems; he may also run classes at the mosque. However, Shi'a Muslims also follow the teachings of religious leaders and thinkers known as ayatollahs.

Islamic Festivals

The main festival celebrated by Muslims throughout the Middle East—and the rest of the Islamic world—is Eid al-Fitr, at the end of the month-long fast of Ramadan in the ninth month of the Islamic year. Another important festival is Eid al-Adha, or the "feast of sacrifice." It falls in the last month of the Islamic year and coincides with the time of pilgrimage to Mecca. Because the Islamic year is based on the lunar calendar, each of the year's twelve months begins when the new moon rises in the night sky. This means the festivals fall at slightly different times each year.

Eid al-Fitr means the "festival of fast-breaking," and it begins at the end of Ramadan, when the new moon appears. Traditions and celebrations may vary from country to country, but for all Muslims, it is the most joyful festival. They go to the mosque to give thanks to Allah and give alms to the poor. Everyone wears their best clothes, visits family and friends, exchanges cards and presents, and prepares special meals. In Egypt, for example, families share picnics and boat trips on the Nile. In Syria, during this and other Islamic festivals, poets compose long, eloquent poems, known as *al-mu'allaqaat*, and hang them on banners across streets for the public to read.

During Eid al-Adha, Muslims recall that the prophet Abraham agreed to sacrifice his own son to Allah. (This story is also recalled in the Jewish and Christian scriptures.) Ultimately, Allah spared the boy, and the people sacrificed a ram in his place. For this reason, Muslims mark this festival with prayers, feasting and the killing of a ram, or other

Iraqi children enjoy the rides at al-Zawraa Park in central Baghdad on the second day of the Eid al-Adha festivities.

Karbala and Najaf

Karbala in southern Iraq is one of the holiest cities of Shi'a Islam. It was there, in 680, that Imam Hussein, grandson of Muhammad, was killed in a battle over the leadership of the Muslim community. The tomb of Hussein is a place of pilgrimage for Shi'a Muslims, second only to Mecca. Many Shi'as hope to be buried in Karbala.

Najaf, also in southern Iraq and a leading center of Islamic scholarship, is the burial place of Ali, father of Hussein. Ali is often seen as the founder of Shi'a Islam.

Karbala and Najaf have had tragic histories. In the early nineteenth century, Hussein's tomb was destroyed by Wahhabi Sunni Muslims. In the 1990s, many thousands of Shi'as in Karbala and Najaf were killed or imprisoned after they rose in rebellion against the repressive regime of Saddam Hussein. Since the overthrow of Saddam Hussein in 2003 by U.S.-led coalition forces, both cities have seen serious conflicts between Shi'a militants and American forces, and, more recently, devastating attacks against the Shi'a by suicide bombers.

animal, in the name of Allah. Some of the meat is eaten within the family, and the rest is given to the poor.

A rather different festival is Ashura, one of the most important events of the year for Shi'a Muslims. Ashura falls on the tenth day of the first month of the Islamic year. On this day, the Shi'a recall the martyrdom of Imam Hussein, son of Ali and grandson of Muhammad. The Shi'a believe that Ali, Hussein, and their descendants were the rightful leaders of the Muslim community. The murder of Ali and the death in battle of Hussein allowed their opponents to claim the leadership, and led to the split in Islam into two main sects—the Sunnis and the Shi'a. For the Shi'a Ashura is a day of mourning and intense emotions, with poetry recitations, chanting and drumming, and the performance of passion plays. Many of the men parade through the streets, symbolically beating themselves to express their grief. In certain Shi'a communities, for example in Lebanon and Iraq, some mourners whip themselves until they bleed. In other communities, such as in Iran, this practice is banned, and red paint is used to symbolize their suffering.

Sunnis and Shi'as

Within the worldwide community of Islam, there are two main groups or sects: the Sunnis and the Shi'as. In core beliefs and religious practices, there is little disagreement between Sunnis and Shi'as. Both use the same Koran, share the same Islamic beliefs, and follow the example of Muhammad.

Sunnis believe that they hold to the traditions of Islam, as taught by Muhammad. The word *Sunni* comes from the Arabic *sunnah*, meaning "tradition or custom." For this reason, the hadith, as well as the Koran, plays a central part in guiding Sunni beliefs and practices. Shi'as also regard the hadith very highly, but their scholars have greater room for interpretation than Sunni scholars do.

Where Sunnis and Shi'as do differ intensely is on the question of leadership. Sunnis believe that the first four Caliphs were the rightfully elected successors of Muhammad. Shi'as believe that Ali, Muhammad's cousin and son-in-law, was Muhammad's chosen successor, and that only direct descendants of Muhammad and of Ali could follow him.

The majority of Muslims today are Sunnis, both worldwide and in the Middle East. An estimated 10–15 percent worldwide are Shi'as. In Middle Eastern countries, the largest numbers of Shi'as are found in Iran, where they make up about 90 percent of the population. In Iraq and Bahrain, they make up more than half the population, and there are also significant numbers of Shi'a Muslims in Lebanon, Yemen, and Kuwait.

The Sunni and Shi'a communities live largely separate lives, coming together only during the hajj and major religious festivals. On the whole, they are tolerant toward one another. However, this tolerance has broken down where there is political instability, for example in Lebanon during the civil war and, more recently, in Iraq. Moreover, most Middle Eastern countries are governed by a Sunni Arab elite. Many Shi'a live in poor communities, with little access to political power and a strong sense of injustice.

Sunnis

With many millions of followers in the Middle East alone, Sunni Islam inevitably has many variations among them. Although Sunnis share the same core beliefs, the religious

The Ayatollahs

The word *ayatollah* means "sign of Allah." It is a title given, by agreement, to a highly respected and learned leader. Ayatollahs are seen as important leaders in their communities and usually have devoted followings.

The role of ayatollah is especially powerful in the Shi'a Islamic Republic of Iran. During the 1980s, all aspects of political and social life in the country were dominated by the supreme spiritual leader, Ayatollah Ruhollah Musavi Khomeini. He became the center of a powerful personality cult, introduced strict Islamic laws, and ruthlessly suppressed any opposition. The current supreme spiritual leader, Ayatollah Khamenei, is a less charismatic figure, but he nevertheless remains very powerful politically.

In Iraq, the overthrow in 2003 of the secular regime of Saddam Hussein, which had favored the minority Sunnis and meted out brutal treatment to many Shi'as, has allowed the return from exile of Ayatollah Sayyid Ali Husayni Sistani. His influence over the Iraqi Shi'as will inevitably play an important part in helping to shape Iraq's future. He has, for example, encouraged all Iraqis to take part in democratic elections.

A photograph of the charismatic religious and political leader Ayatollah Khomeini, taken in 1979 in Tehran, Iran.

understanding and daily practices of, for example, a poor, uneducated Yemeni farmer, a learned Egyptian scholar, and a wealthy Saudi businessman may be very different.

Some Sunni Muslims follow a very strict interpretation of Islam. The Salafi movement, also known as Wahhabism, is one example of a strict Sunni group.

Wahhabis

In eighteenth-century Arabia, a Sunni scholar, Muhammad ibn Abd al-Wahhab, felt that many Muslims had strayed from the true path of Islam. He and his followers sought a pure form of the faith, believing that true Muslims should live exactly as Muhammad and his early successors did. This meant living simply and without luxury, and following strict religious practices. These included a ban on praying to saints; going on pilgrimage to holy sites such as tombs; and specific religious festivals, such as celebration of the Prophet Muhammad's birthday.

The Salafis

Today, Sunni Muslims who have been influenced by the teachings of Muhammad ibn Abd al-Wahhab are more commonly referred to as Salafis. Different Salafi groups and Salafi-influenced political parties extend throughout the

Wahhabis in Saudi Arabia

When the powerful al-Saud family (the dynasty that currently rules Saudi Arabia) began to practice Wahhabism, they used it to help them establish control over much of the Arabian Peninsula. The al-Saudi kingdom of Saudi Arabia made Wahhabism the state religion. Toward the end of the twentieth century, the influence of the Wahhabi Saudis throughout the Middle East was strengthened by huge oil wealth and control of the holy cities of Mecca and Medina. In addition, they have used oil money to promote Wahhabism worldwide, through religious schools and the Arabic-language media.

Wahhabism touches every aspect of life in Saudi Arabia. No religion other than Islam is publicly allowed. Acohol and tobacco are forbidden; movies are banned; and all Saudis are expected to follow a strict code of behavior and dress. In public life, women are largely segregated from men, and their freedoms are greatly restricted.

Middle East. All follow a strict, **fundamentalist** form of Islam. The majority of these groups are peaceful, but some groups are more extreme, and a few are violent. These groups, known as jihadists, advocate Islamic holy war, or jihad.

The more extreme Salafi groups have also been influenced by the radical Egyptian scholar Sayyid Qutb. Qutb is often called the "father of modern fundamentalism." His interpretation of the Koran is an extreme one that argues for a form of jihad that the vast majority of Muslims reject. Writing from prison in the 1950s, he attacked the Western way of life; both Christianity and Judaism; and most Islamic rulers in the Middle East, whom he regarded as corrupt and impure Muslims.

Yemeni Salafis

"They believe they are correct and that everyone else is wrong. . . . They follow the words and actions of the Prophet step-by-step. They do not accept changes or modernizations. . . . They are closed to the world. They do not read books or newspapers. They are not very interested in culture. They have no idea about technology."

Bassam Jameel al Saqqaf, journalist with the English-speaking Yemen Times, *on Salafis in Yemen.*

The Muslim Brotherhood

For many Muslims, politics and religion are often inextricably linked. Nevertheless, the majority of Middle Eastern states have had largely secular governments. The Muslim Brotherhood, founded in Egypt in the 1920s, argued that, in an Islamic country, the whole of society—including the government— should be run according to strict Islamic principles. The Brotherhood spread to other Middle Eastern countries including Syria and Jordan, as well as the Palestinian territories (where it became Hamas). The Brotherhood has often come into violent conflict with the established government. In the 1980s, an uprising in Syria led by the Muslim Brotherhood was put down by the Assad regime with such brutal force that more than twenty thousand people lost their lives.

Shi'a Sects and Divisions

There are several distinct sects among the Shi'as. The divisions are made according to which of the direct male descendants of Ali, (the fourth caliph and son-in-law of Muhammad), known as the imams, a particular group follows.

The Twelvers, the Seveners, and the Fivers

The vast majority of Shi'as belong to the Imami, or Twelver, sect. They believe that there were twelve rightful descendants of Muhammad in his role as political and spiritual leader of Islam. According to the Imamis, the twelfth of these, known as the Hidden Imam, never died but went to a place beyond the physical world. Imami Shi'ism is found through much of the Middle East but is dominant in Iran, where it is the official religion. It is also a potent force in Iraq and parts of Lebanon.

The Ismailis, or Seveners, are followers of the seventh imam, Ismail. Once politically powerful, this group has only small numbers in the Middle East, notably in Syria and Yemen. The Zaydis, or Fivers, are followers of the fifth imam. They are found mostly in Yemen.

Crossing the Line

"If any Druze girl marries another religion, she's totally forbidden from her society, maybe also her family. That's the only problem I found with Druze society — they are good people; they love everyone. But when it comes to religion, there's a red line that can't be crossed."

Mazen, a nineteen-year-old Greek Orthodox Christian in Lebanon.

The Alawites

The majority of Alawites are found in Syria, where they form the largest religious minority. Another several thousand Alawites also reside in Lebanon. Many Muslims do not accept the Alawites as part of the worldwide Muslim community. Alawite beliefs are said to be close to those of the Ismaili Shi'ahs, but because they keep many aspects of their faith secret, do not accept converts, or publish their religious texts, it is difficult for outsiders to interpret their beliefs.

For hundreds of years, Alawites lived in poor, isolated communities. Some Alawites sought to raise their status by joining the Syrian army. It was in this way that Hafez Assad seized power in 1970. Assad ruled Syria with an iron grip for thirty years and built a power base of loyal, unquestioning Alawites around him. In Syria, today, although the Alawites are a minority, they continue to be politically powerful, particularly in the Syrian army and the intelligence services.

The Druze

Significant Druze communities are found in Syria and Lebanon, and smaller numbers can be found in Israel and Jordan. In Lebanon, the Druze make up an estimated 6 percent of the total population and have played a significant part in the country's history.

An elderly Druze mourner attends a funeral in the northern Israeli Druze village of Maghar.

The Druze sect probably had its origins in Ismaili Islam. Persecuted for their beliefs, the Druze found sanctuary in the mountains of Lebanon and Syria. There, they developed as close-knit, independent communities, largely isolated from the outside world. The Druze have often come into bitter conflict with a similarly close-knit independent community, the Christian Maronites.

The Druze call themselves Muslims, but their beliefs and practices have developed very differently from mainstream Islam. Most Muslims regard Druze beliefs as heretical. Like the Ismailis and the Alawites, the Druze are secretive about their beliefs and practices. They do not allow converts to their faith, and marriage to non-Druze is forbidden.

CHAPTER 5

Religions Today and Tomorrow

For hundreds of years, members of the three major faiths shared the lands of the Middle East. They often came into conflict, but they also learned to live alongside one another. However, since the establishment of Israel in 1948, the 1991 Gulf War, and the U.S.-led invasion of Iraq in 2003, there has been an ever widening gulf between the faiths.

Islam has long been the main faith of the Middle Eastern people. More than 85 percent are practicing Muslims. But even as minority faiths, Judaism and Christianity have continued to make a rich cultural contribution to the region. Today, however, there is a danger that many of the region's ancient Jewish groups outside of Israel and Christian communities may die out altogether. In Iraq, for example, thousands have left the Christian community over the last twenty years and more are leaving now because of anti-Christian attacks. In the Palestinian territories, life for Palestinians, whether Muslim or Christian, has become increasingly difficult in recent years as a result of Israeli occupation, conflict, economic decline, curfews, and general insecurity. More and more Palestinian Christians, almost all Arabs, are leaving to seek a better life in the West.

Although the vast majority of Middle Eastern Muslims are moderate and peace-loving, there is a growing segment within Islam that advocates violence. Sometimes this manifests itself as being anti-Israeli, anti-Western, and anti-Christian, but it also reflects divisions within Islam. Nowhere is this more evident than in Iraq.

The Future of Jerusalem

Jerusalem is a city sacred to all three faiths and long a place of pilgrimage. It is sacred to Jews as the ancient site of King Solomon's Temple. Christians believe it was in Jerusalem that Jesus Christ was crucified and rose from the dead. Muslims believe that Muhammad ascended into heaven from a site in Jerusalem.

Today, Jerusalem, often a source of conflict in the past, is at the heart of the Israeli-Palestinian conflict. The Israelis claim the whole of Jerusalem as their capital; the Palestinians claim the eastern Arab part. Religious attachments to major holy sites often increase the divide between the faiths. The most sensitive sites are those on the hill known as Temple Mount, where the Al-Aqsa Mosque is said to have been built on the site of the ancient Jewish Temple.

There are many different groups, with different motivations, contributing to the continuing terrible violence in Iraq. It is clear, however, that religious extremism plays a central part in this. The Sunni minority fears that, in the future, Iraq will be controlled by a Shi'a Islamic system of government. Many of the most violent attacks and suicide bombings have been carried out by Sunni extremists, such as al-Qaeda in Iraq. These include both Iraqis and foreign "jihadi" fighters, seen by al-Qaeda as a worldwide vanguard of a global, pan-Islamic uprising.

A Peaceful Majority

While religious tensions remain high in many Middle Eastern countries, both between religions and within religious divisions, the majority of people in the region are not fanatics. They hope for peace and stability and both religious and political freedom. For centuries the three great religions have coexisted in this region. It remains to be seen whether moderate Middle Easterners will be able to resist the pressure of extremists who often use religion to further political ends.

TIME LINE

c. 3000 B.C. Phoenicians develop first-known alphabet and establish some of the earliest towns and city states.

c. 3000 B.C. – c. 300 B.C. Much of Middle East under the control of different empires: Ancient Egypt, Assyria, Babylon, and Persia.

c. 2000 B.C. Birth of Abraham, prophet of all three faiths; regarded as the founder of the Jewish people.

c. 628 B.C.–551 B.C. The prophet Zoroaster, founder of Zoroastrianism, born in Persia.

588 B.C. Kingdom of Judah is overthrown by the Chaldeans and many Jews are deported to Babylon.

538 B.C. Jews in Babylon are allowed to return to Judah.

300 B.C.–A.D. 400 Much of Middle East controlled by Greek and, later, Roman Empires.

c. 6 B.C.–c A.D. 30 Lifetime of Jesus Christ.

c. A.D. 30 First Christian churches founded; writing of Christian New Testament begins.

A.D. 70 Expulsion of Jews from Judaea by ancient Romans.

313 Roman Emperor Constantine converted to Christianity; beginning of spread of Christianity throughout Roman Empire.

570–632 Lifetime of Muhammad, founder of Islam.

600s Islam spreads throughout Middle East and North Africa.

661 Death of Ali, fourth Muslim Caliph; beginning of decisive split between Sunni and Shi'a Muslims.

680 Imam Hussein, grandson of the Prophet Muhammad, is killed in battle at Karbala.

1054 the Great Schism; split of the Christian church: eastern part becomes the Orthodox Church; western part becomes Roman Catholic.

1517 Reformation in western Christian Church divides it into Catholic and Protestant denominations.

1932 The Saudi Wahhabi state oficially becomes the Kingdom of Saudi Arabia.

1939–1945 World War II; Nazi Holocaust kills six million Jews.

1948 State of Israel is founded.

1970s Hafez Assad seizes power in Syria. Alawite Muslims become politically powerful.

1975–1991 Lebanese Civil War. Christian Maronites and Lebanese Muslims (particularly the Druze) come into conflict.

1979 Ayatollah Khomeini returns from exile and becomes the spiritual and political leader of Iran.

1991 Gulf War drives invading Iraqi army out of Kuwait.

2003 U.S-led invasion of Iraq.

GLOSSARY

ascension: Christian belief that Jesus Christ rose to heaven to be reunited with God the Father

ayatollah: important religious leader of the Shi'a Muslims

baptize: to plunge someone in water in order to purify them or initiate them

Caliphs: successors to Muhammad and leaders of the Muslim community, responsible for ensuring that people lived according to the Koran

conversion: the changing of one's beliefs and the acceptance of a new religion

covenant: a binding promise or contract

crucifixion: death by hanging on a cross

denomination: group within, or branch of, a larger religious group

Diaspora: the movement of Jewish people away from ancient Palestine (the "Promised Land"), to settle in other parts of the world

disciple: someone who follows and believes in a religious leader; one of the first twelve men who followed Jesus Christ

Eucharist: special act of worship during Christian religious services, also called Holy Communion; known as Mass in the Roman Catholic Church and holy liturgy in Orthodox churches

evangelical: having to do with the belief that one should try to persuade as many people as possible to convert to one's faith; usually refers to particular Christian denominations

Fertile Crescent: large area of fertile land in the Middle East, reaching from the Tigris and Euphrates Rivers (modern-day Iraq and Syria) through to Israel and Egypt

fundamentalist: person who follows religious laws very strictly

ghetto: a part of a city where a certain ethnic or religious group is forced to live, either by necessity or by law

heretical: not conforming to the teachings of a particular religion and is rejected as incorrect

hermit: person who lives a solitary and simple life, usually for religious reasons

Holocaust: the killing of millions of Jews and others by the Nazis in World War II

idol: image or statue that is worshipped as a god

imam: Muslim prayer leader and religious teacher; also used in Shi'a Islam as a title, referring to the leaders the Shi'a believe to be Muhammad's descendants and rightful successors

matzo: a brittle type of flat bread, made without yeast

GLOSSARY

Mesopotamian provinces: the lowlands watered by the Tigris and Euphrates rivers, now the state of Iraq

Messiah: "anointed one"; in Judaism, a leader who will be sent by God to bring peace to the world; in Christianity, the Son of God, Jesus Christ

missionary: a person who travels to another country to convert the local people to his or her own religion

monotheistic: having to do with the belief that there is only one God

mosque: Muslim building for public worship

Ottoman Empire: the empire of the Ottoman Turks, which lasted over 600 years (1299-1922), and which included all of the Middle East except Iran and the desert interior of Arabia

pagan: having to do with ancient religious beliefs, in which each natural element has its own god

patriarch: a male leader of a family or group

pilgrim: person who journeys to a holy place associated with a religious leader

polytheistic: having to do with the belief that there is more than one god

precarious: issecure or uncertain

prophet: someone through whom God is said to speak; often called "messenger" in Islam

rabbi: Jewish teacher and spiritual leader

Reformation: radical reform in the western Christian Church in the sixteenth century that led to the founding of the Protestant Churches

resurrection: rising from the dead; (capitalized) the rising of Jesus from the dead

revelation: powerful experience that is believed to be a message from God

scripture: religious or sacred book or piece of writing

sect: religious group that has split from the main religion; an independent religious movement

secular: not religious

synagogue: a Jewish place of worship

Zionist: having to do with the political movement that aimed at founding a Jewish state in Palestine

Websites

BBC News: Middle East
   www.bbc.co.uk/religion
BBC World Service/Religions of the World
   www.bbc.co.uk/worldservice/people/features/world_religions/
Global Connections: The Middle East—Religions
   www.pbs.org/wgbh/globalconnections/mideast/themes/religion/index.html
The Library of Congress Country Studies
   http://lcweb2.loc.gov/frd/cs
The Middle East Information Network
   www.mideastinfo.com

Note to educators and parents: The publisher has carefully reviewed these Web sites to ensure that they are suitable for children. Many Web sites change frequently, however, and Gareth Stevens, Inc., cannot guarantee that a site's future contents will continue to meet our high standards of quality and educational value. Be advised that children should be closely supervised whenever they access the Internet.

Books

Buller, Laura. *A Faith Like Mine: A Celebration of the World's Religions as Seen Through the Eyes of Children*. Dorling Kindersley, 2005.
Gunderson, Cory. *Religions of the Middle East*. (World in Conflict—the Middle East) ABDO Publishing, 2003.
Langley, Myrtle. *Eyewitness: Religions*. Eyewitness Books. Dorling Kindersley, 2003.
Religions of the World (series). World Almanac Library, 2006.
World Faiths (series). Houghton Mifflin, 2005.

ABOUT THE AUTHOR

Gill Stacey is an educational writer and editor with a background in teaching and publishing in the developing world. She has traveled extensively in Africa, the Middle East, South Asia, and Europe, and has written many non fiction books for children.

ABOUT THE CONSULTANT

William Ochsenwald is Professor of History at Virginia Polytechnic Institute and State University. He is author of *The Middle East: A History*, a textbook now in its sixth edition. Professor Ochsenwald has also written many other books and articles dealing with the history of the Middle East.

INDEX

Page numbers in **bold** indicate illustrations.